magnificent Normandy

Photos Franck Godard
Original text Olivier Bouteiller
Translation Jacqui Taylor

Origination and editorial direction Bertrand Dalin

Cover photo - That characteristic sound of surf and seagulls' cries; the waves of the endless Channel lap the shore. Water round your ankles and sand tickling the soles of your feet give you a delightful feeling of freedom. It looks great, it's good for you - it's Normandy!

Summary

Previous page - Gap in the clouds
— and the ocean is bathed in
a superb crescent of golden light.

Twilight, often a moment of inspiration
for the Normandy Impressionists.

Editorial

From the Côte d'Albâtre (Alabaster Coast), cradle of Impressionism, to Millet's Cotentin and Poussin's Andelys, Normandy has always inspired painters. The region is a palette of colours all to itself.

The fields make up a many-coloured mosaic pattern, earth-brown and soft or deep green, yellow squares of wheat ears in the sun, linen-blue with grains of tiger's-eye in bloom. A patchwork as far as the eye can see, to the edge of forests like huge emerald caskets. Green pastures plunge down the sides of cliffs, chalk-white, flint-grey and ochre with clay, towards the sea which is deep marine-blue or turquoise depending on the mood of the weather. Not forgetting the yellow flag on thatched roofs, the snowy balls of apple-blossom with their pink anthers, the hydrangeas — white, violet, amethyst — and Monet's water lilies under the gaze of the weeping willows.

'This is one of those delightful corners of the earth which hold a sensual charm for the eyes', said Guy de Maupassant, of his region.

Isn't Normandy magnificent?

Previous page - Brown sand striped with water is uncovered as the tide goes out.

Norman atmosphere. A bronze-and-silver sky is mirrored in the glittering wavelets come to lap the ochre beach at Cabourg.

History

The first human traces found on what is today Norman territory go back to 500 000 B.C. At first, it was a sparsely-populated region inhabited by Celts, invested by one of Caesar's lieutenants in 56 B.C.

The Seine was then used to transport tin from Cornouailles. During the Gallo-Roman era, two large and already prosperous towns grew up around the Norman Vexin; Rotomagus (Rouen) and in Caux country, Juliobona (Lillebonne).

In the IVth century the Empire was reorganised. Western Neustria, the future Normandy, was divided into several cities: Evreux, Lisieux, Bayeux, Sées, Coutances, and Avranches, with Rouen as their capital.

Previous page - At the age of eight, Guillaume the Bastard became Duke of Normandy, then William the Conqueror. In 1066 he beat the English at Hastings. As King of England, he was more powerful than the King of France when he was crowned on Christmas Day in Westminster Abbey.

The Gallo-Roman theatre-amphitheatre at Lillebonne (then Juliobona), capital of the Caletes. This people of ancient Gaul occupied what is now the Caux country, in the first and second centuries A.D.

Saint Wandrilles' Abbey, founded in the VIIth century by Saint Wandrille, minister to King Dagobert.

Following page - The drakkar, or Viking longship, got its name from the dragon's head on its prow. The Vikings confronted the seas aboard langskips and knörrs, boats which allowed them to navigate in all weathers.

The first monasteries built in the VIth century were symbols of wealth coveted by the barbarians. The Francs occupied the territory towards 800 A.D. and the Vikings also made attempts to conquer it, despite Charlemagne's efforts to protect the hills and fortified bridges set up across the rivers by Charles the Bald.

The Northmen rushed into the Seine estuary with their longships, and sacked the land. Countless abbeys were pillaged, if not totally destroyed, and towns were devastated. These strandhögg, or attacks on the banks, were repeated many times along all the coasts as far as Northern Cotentin, and are retraced by Guillaume de Jumièges who wrote in the XIth century: 'There is not even one dog left to bark at their heels'. In 911, the King of France, Charles the Simple, handed over the region to the Viking chief Rollo, in a treaty signed at Saint-Clair-sur-Epte near Gisors, sealing the birth of the Duchy of Normandy in exchange for peace. Although pagan, of course, Rollo had himself baptised in 912. With the rebuilding of the abbeys, the region was soon considered to be the richest province in France.

The Normans continued their roughing-up as far as Italy and the Holy Land during the reign of Richard the Magnificent. In 1035, his heir Guillaume (or William) became Duke of Normandy, and in 1066, left with a fleet of more than 1 000 ships from Dives-sur-Mer to attack the English, defeat them at Hastings and become King of England.

These events are retraced in the famous Bayeux Tapestry, both work of art and historical document. On the death of William the Conqueror in 1087, the rivalry among his heirs led to fratricidal war.

In the XIIth century, Normandy became part of the Plantagenet empire, on the marriage of Henry I's only daughter, who had survived a shipwreck.

Previous page - Row of half-timbered and thatched houses in the Rue Eau-de-Robec in Rouen; a style of building typical of the region.

The Château de Saint-Germain-de-Livet, surrounded by the River Touques. Two interesting architectural styles: one XVth century, in wood, the other, a XVIth century brick-and-stone draughtboard.

Ruins of Richard the Lionheart's 'year-old daughter' Château-Gaillard, impressive medieval fortress built in twelve months to protect Rouen and its surroundings from the King of France, Philippe Auguste.

Following page
Above - The elegant Château de Martainville, built in Seine-Maritime at the end of the XVth century, is now a listed building, and contains the Museum of Norman Arts and Traditions.

Below - Last medieval remains: the Château de Tourelles at Vernon, near the Vieux Moulin (Old Windmill). It was used to defend the city, border between the duchy of Normandy and the kingdom of France.

After the reigns of Richard the Lionheart and his brother John, Dukes of Normandy and Kings of England, Philippe-Auguste joined the duchy to the kingdom of France in 1204, and signed the Treaty of Paris on 4 December 1259, by which Henry III abandoned his rights to several provinces, including Normandy.

Despite this, the Exchequer, sovereign legal and financial court established under Henry I, lingered on, and was even confirmed by the Norman Charter signed in 1315 by Louis X le Hutin (the Quarreller), which guaranteed freedom and autonomy to the regional population.

After a long period of peace, history repeated itself, and Normandy became a strategic stake in the Hundred Years' War. In 1346, Edward III of England landed in the Cotentin via Saint-Vaast-la-Hougue, and invaded the territory, ending its prosperity. It was the beginning of endless conflict between Normans and English.

Close-up of Bayeux Cathedral, consecrated in the presence of William the Conqueror on 14 July 1077.

Castle keep of the Château Bouvreuil, built in Rouen by Philippe Auguste and known as Joan of Arc's Tower, for her trial took place here.

Following page - The white stone statue of François I, put up in tribute to Le Havre's founding father, contrasts with an azure sky.

In 1415, Henry V of England arrived with his army at the Touques estuary and overran Caen, Bayeux, Argentan, Evreux and Falaise, then laid siege to Rouen early in 1419. It is here, under English domination, that Joan of Arc was burnt alive on 30 May 1431, almost a year after her capture and an unrelenting trial conducted by Bishop Cauchon who was hoping the English would give him the archbishopric of Rouen. Several months later, the Duke of Bedford created a university at Caen.

The territory was progressively taken back by Charles VII until 1450, with popular support, but Normandy came out of this occupation impoverished, and the Bishop of Lisieux wrote that this 'formerly glorious land' was left 'totally abandoned, looking like a desert'.

In 1469, the duchy acquired its definitive status of French province. In 1515, François I transformed the Exchequer into the Rouen Parliament, and decided to found Le Havre in 1517.

FRANÇOIS, PAR LA GRACE DE DIEU,
ROY DE FRANCE , ORDONNONS ,

pour tenir en seureté les navires et vaisseaux
... nos subjectz navigans en ...
... havre ...

The Reformation led to further conflict between the Huguenots, supported by the English, and the Norman Catholics. Catherine de Medicis was there in person at the recapture of Rouen and Le Havre in 1564. In 1589, the Huguenot Henri of Navarre, later King Henry IV, defeated the Catholic Duc de Mayenne at Arques-la-Bataille near Dieppe.

A period of economic growth began at this time, with Norman sailors and explorers covering the globe. Jacques Cartier had already sailed for Canada the previous century; now Samuel Champion left Normandy for 'New France'. Colbert and Vauban enriched ports and towns with their architectural improvements.

The Revolution arrived: the Normans supported the Chouans and the Girondins, whose members of parliament had been arrested, thus provoking the uprising. Several Norman towns were threatened by the Comte de Frotté's Royalist troops. The Comte was later executed by Napoleon's soldiers.

Previous page -The arrival of fleets of tall ships in the Rouen docks recalls the age-old Norman maritime tradition. For centuries, Normandy has been a departure point for expeditions on all the high seas of the globe.

Statue of Pléville-Lepelley, a corsair from Granville, put up in 1907. The buccaneer was born in 1726, lost a leg in naval fighting at 18, then went on to become Commander of the port of Marseilles under Louis XVI and Naval Minister during the post-revolutionary Directoire.

Tribute paid to the aviators Nungesser and Coli, on the wall of their museum at Etretat. They witnessed the technical progress of the early XXth century, and took their first steps in aeronautics trying to fly the Atlantic on 8 May 1927 aboard their plane White Bird. They were last seen from the cliffs of Etretat.

Following page - The 1923 boardwalk at Deauville, made of exotic azobe wood, stretches over 643 metres near the bathing huts bearing the names of film stars who've been to the American Film Festival.

In 1790, Normandy was reorganised into five departments by the National Assembly. Three years later, Normandy-born Charlotte Corday, from Sées in the Orne, assassinated Marat in his bathtub.

In 1843, Rouen was the first French town to be linked to Paris by the railway, which launched the industrial age in Normandy. Agriculture was thriving, and there was a corresponding boom in the textile and metallurgy sectors, naval construction and later the car industry. Sea bathing became very popular at the end of the XIXth century, which made tourism an important new economic sector.

The region was hard-hit by war again, and saw the arrival of the Prussians this time, in 1815 and 1870. Despite the tough battles fought in Normandy, many Alsatians chose to settle there when Alsace and Lorraine were ceded to Germany.

A fine view of Arromanches from the cliffs, with the remains of the artificial port Mulberry B, set up over 12 kilometres in ten days for the Normandy Landings.

In front of the Town Hall, the stone marking freedom for Sainte-Mère-Eglise, first village to be liberated in France in 1944. The parachutist John Steele won fame by getting stuck on the church spire while attempting to land.

During the Second World War, Normandy paid a heavy toll again, from 1940 onwards. Many towns were destroyed, even completely wiped out. Though the British attempt to help failed at Dieppe in 1942, the word 'Normandy' will always stand for liberation because 135 000 men and 20 000 vehicles landed on beaches called Utah, Omaha, Gold, Juno and Sword, in the Cotentin, in the early hours of Tuesday 6 June 1944.

The battle of Normandy went on until 21 August, involving American, British and Canadian Allies who arrived by sea and by air. The fall of Cherbourg freed the first major port for Allied ships to dock in, and progressively, the German troops were pushed back. Whole towns were more or less wiped off the map, such as Saint-Lô, Flers, Le Havre and Caen. It took years for them all to rise again from the ruins and rubble.

The stirring 60th D-Day anniversary commemoration in 2004 testifies to that national and international collective memory which stands forever against Nazi barbarity.

Pointe du Hoc, and the road leading to the bunker on the cliff-edge. The craters are still here, as proof of the intensity of the bombing. A granite column has been put up in memory of the 2nd battalion of Rangers who scaled 30 metres of rocks in June 1944 to occupy these heights.

Emotion and contemplation, while recalling those lives given for freedom on the Normandy beaches.

Normandy was split into two regions in 1973; Upper (Haute) Normandy, containing the Seine-Maritime and Eure departments, and Lower (Basse) Normandy, with the three departments Calvados, Manche and Orne.

Today, a few politicians would like a return to one region, sole and whole against Europe and the world. There is some grinding of teeth and a certain conservatism, even if the Pont de Normandie has bridged the Seine since 1995, thrown like a ribbon between its two banks, and in some places, such as the universities, frontiers and divisions have long since vanished.

The Norway (ex-France) on its way out of Le Havre. Though transformed and re-named, those powerful foghorns echoing through the town still bring a lump to the throats of its citizens. In the grip of nostalgia...

Following page - The Pont de Normandie is an architectural marvel, and was the longest cable-stayed bridge in the world in 1995, proud of its 2 141 metres spanning the Seine, linking Le Havre to Honfleur. Only the principal reach of the Tatara Bridge in Japan, opened in 1999, is longer.

Towns and Villages

In the north of the region, the River Bresle forms a natural border with the Somme, in Picardy. On the Côte d'Albâtre, the highest cliffs in Europe soar upwards as far as Le Havre. Here, they offer an exceptional panoramic view, from the Terrasses site and the Calvaire des Marins (Sailors' Cross), over the ancient Cordiers quarter, where fishermen didn't think twice about spending the summer crowded into the basements of their homes, which they let out to visitors.

Eu welcomes hikers following the Bresle. This historic town is known as the oldest of the region and the last royal estate in France, and contains many listed sites and monuments, including the Louis-Philippe museum. It is at the junction of the Ivory and Spice Roads, and the Glass Road, glass being a speciality of the whole valley.

Previous page - At Le Havre, the straight lines of Perret's architecture are broken by the Volcan's curves. This cultural centre was built in 1982 from Oscar Niemeyer's plans. In the background is the tower of Saint Joseph's Church, a monumental concrete building, whose silhouette is anchored in the landscape.

Londinières, charming village above Neufchâtel-en-Bray, nestling in the green hollow of the Seine-Maritime hills. The Roman road used to pass through this spot, going straight to Dieppe.

The Three Graces *play in their fountain at Forges-les-Eaux. They symbolise the three springs flowing in the town, and were sculpted by Jean-Marc Depas in 1999.*

Following page
Above - View of the town, the seafront and the open sea from the heights of Dieppe, bathed in wonderful light.

Below - Georges Braque's tomb at Varangeville-sur-Mer, close to Dieppe. The artist's creativity left its mark on XXth century painting.

Towards the south-east, on one of the banks of the Béthune, Neufchâtel-en-Bray and its half-timbered houses jealously keep the secret of their heart-shaped cheeses. The earth here was rich in iron in Gallo-Roman times, and the spring water considered to be therapeutic, so the name Forges-les-Eaux was an obvious choice. This town, perched 175 metres up above the Thérain valley in the Bray country, is also famous for its pottery, manufactured until the end of the XIXth century. Today, superb examples can be seen in the museum. In the south of the department, in 1848, Ry was the scene of a trivial local drama which inspired Gustave Flaubert to write Madame Bovary.

A fair number of explorers took sail from Dieppe in the XIVth and XVth centuries, but it was in the XVIth century that they brought back the ivory which was to contribute to its expansion. This delightful town is one of the Seine-Maritime's two sous-préfectures and an important fishing port (traditionally, the fishermen gather in the Pollet quarter). Sole, sea-bass, turbot and scallops can be tasted after a visit to the Cité de la Mer, whose godmother is Anita Conti, the first female oceanographer.

GEORGES BRAQUE
1882 PEINTRE 1963

MARCELLE BRAQUE
1879 – 1965

In the sailors' cemetery at Varengeville, the painter Georges Braque is buried close to the church, against the side of the cliff. The lighthouse keeps a look-out from the Ailly headland. From valley to valley, from the Saâne to the Dun, one peaceful village follows another. The smallest river in France flows through Veules-les-Roses and on to the Channel, its 1 100 metres dotted with watermills. Neighbouring Saint-Valery-en-Caux contains two treasures: a Henri IV house and the Penitents' Cloister.

Going further down, the visitor can daydream in the English-style park at the Château de Cany-Barville, and again in front of Sassetot-le-Mauconduit, the castle where Sissi, Empress of Austria, stayed in the summer of 1875.

Previous page
Above - Calm sea and misty sky at sunrise:
the pleasure craft catch high tide and
sail out of port at Saint-Valery-en-Caux.

Below - Le Tréport, most northerly town
in Normandy at the mouth of the Bresle.
Saint-Jacques' Church watches over
the colourful houses along the quay.

Henri IV house at Saint-Valery-en-Caux,
on the Quai de la Batellerie. It was built
in the XVIth century by the shipowner
Guillaume Ladiré. The sculptures
decorating its front recall his
boats' expeditions to Brazil.

*Caux cows between green pasture
and blue waves: Normandy's colours.*

*Following page
Above - At Fécamp, the wooden
landing-stages in pitch pine and azobe
are a favourite place to stroll.
The oldest dates back to 1899.*

*Below - The Benedictine Palace is a
splendid stone-and-brick building begun
in 1863, with carving and a monumental
staircase. Its founder Alexandre le Grand
wanted to merge art and industry
in this distillery, where the famous
liqueur is made.*

There are lots of small harbours along the coast, as far as the terre-neuvas country. Fécamp's link with the sea goes back to the time when 'sea-convicts' went fishing for cod off the far-away frozen Canadian coast, and a museum is devoted to these brave seekers of 'white gold'. On the cliffs, the sailor's footpath, or Côte de la Vierge, leads to the chapel of Notre-Dame-du-Salut and the semaphore, and a sweeping view of the town.

Fécamp contains the majestic Benedictine Palace built by Alexandre le Grand, the abbey church of the Trinité whose relic of the Precious Blood still attracts pilgrims, and the remains of the ducal palace put up for Henry II Plantagenet.

Round about Fécamp, between fields and sea, nestle those charming villages dear to the heart of Guy de Maupassant: Goderville, Fauville, Bréauté and Epreville, whose aubergiste (landlord) was 'Maître Chicot'.

He was fond of Etretat too, where he had the 'Guillette' built. The author knew every corner of 'l'Aiguille creuse' where crime writer Maurice Leblanc sent his Arsène Lupin. The world's tourists are thrilled to discover this finger of rock pointing up to the sky from behind an arch sculpted in the chalk and flint of the cliff.

*The famous chalk needle, 51 metres high.
Victor Hugo wrote of the Etretat cliffs:
'This is the greatest architecture
there can be.'*

*Following page - The famous Etretat
pebble beach is part of the site's identity,
as are the cliffs and the fishing dories.*

'What I saw at Etretat is admirable. The cliff is pierced from place to place by great natural arches under which the sea beats with the tide' wrote Victor Hugo.

Etretat has other charms, however, such as some fine residences nestling in greenery.

Coloured dories with their sturdy wooden hulls, resistant to all weathers and to beaching on pebbles. Etretat was a fishing village before becoming a seaside resort.

*Following page
Above - Etretat and its cliffs, bathed in the light of the setting sun. This happens every evening, but is never quite the same, nor totally different, twice-running.*

Below - The chapel of Notre-Dame-de-la-Garde was built in 1854 on top of the cliff, in homage to sailors. It was destroyed during the Occupation, and rebuilt in 1950.

Previous double-spread - Notre-Dame Cathedral in Rouen seems to watch over the sleeping town, crossed by the languorous Seine with its bridges like hyphens linking left bank to right.

Church of Sainte-Jeanne-d'Arc, Place du Vieux-Marché in Rouen, built of stone and slate in the modern style and consecrated in 1979.

Following page - The Gros-Horloge, or Great Clock, and the Pavillon des Cadrans, architectural jewel on the arch across the pedestrian street near the belfry and the former Town Hall.

It was Victor Hugo again who wrote in Autumn Leaves that Rouen is 'the town of a hundred bell towers chiming in the air'. The 'prefecture' (administrative capital) of Seine-Maritime is split in two by the river On the right bank, some carefully-preserved architectural wonders and medieval buildings recall Rouen's XVIII century importance as second French town. In his *Mémoires d'un touriste* Stendhal exclaimed 'What is admirable in Rouen is that the walls of all the houses are made from large pieces of wood placed vertically a foot apart'.

They can be found in the Beauvoisine, Saint-Maclou and Saint-Vivien quarters, towards the Rue Cauchoise, the Rue Beffroy and the picturesque Rue Eau-de-Robec. Houses and mansions recall the drapers, renowned in Rouen, as were stained-glass and pottery-making. The cathedral, painted 30 times by Claude Monet, has a 151 metre spire, the highest in France.

The Place du Vieux-Marché has hosted more than the market in its time. It was the scene of public executions, the most famous being Joan of Arc's. She was burned alive in 1431, while Rouen was in the hands of the English.

Apart from the church and the street that bear her name, there is also the Tour Jeanne d'Arc. Put up in 1204, this tower was Rouen's castle keep before becoming Joan of Arc's cell. The Palais de Justice with its main body and two carved stone wings is an impressive vestige of the flamboyant style, and is one of the local architectural treasures.

Among these are the remains of the city walls towards the Boulevards de l'Yser and de Verdun, and the Porte Guillaume-Lion on the Quai de Paris, the last of the 19 gates which protected Rouen in the reign of Philippe-Auguste. Close by, the ruins of the Augustinian convent are sheltered by a garden.

Several historical buildings now house schools and administrative departments, such as the the 'Ecole régionale des beaux-arts', or Fine-Arts school (former Saint-Maclou ossuary with its macabre frescos) and the Préfecture (formerly the Hôtel-Dieu). Pierre Corneille, who was born in Rouen, overlooks his town from the plinth of David d'Angers statue on the square in front of the Arts Theatre. A second bronze sculpture lords it over the courtyard of the Jesuit college, while Gustave Flaubert stands proudly on the Place des Carmes.

Previous page - The breathtaking spire of Rouen Cathedral challenges the sky. Its 151 metres make it the highest in France.

The tall and venerable XVth to XVIIIth century buildings around the Place de la Pucelle mingle four centuries of atmosphere in the square.

Peaceful atmosphere in the Seine valley. Saint-Martin-de-Boscherville and Saint George's Abbey watch the river flow by.

Following page
Above - The elegant Vacquerie house at Villequier, named after the long-voyage captain who had it built. Victor Hugo stayed here as a member of the family from 1839 onwards, when the younger Vacquerie son married Léopoldine Hugo. Today, the house is a museum to the famous author.

Below - At the entrance to Le Havre, massive Graville Priory proudly overlooks the town. The abbey's benefactor was Lord Guillaume de Malet, one of William the Conqueror's companions-in-arms at Hastings.

Along the Seine, near Caudebec-en-Caux, Villequier remembers Victor Hugo and his daughter Léopoldine, drowned in the river. She is buried in the cemetery of this small village.

On evening's golden hues I shall not gaze,
Nor on the vessels that to Harfleur come;
But my quest o'er, upon thy grave shall place
A wreath of holly green, and heather bloom.
(*Tomorrow at dawn*, in *Contemplations*).

The monks had marvellous abbeys built in the river bends. Their route crosses Normandy, passing through Saint-Georges-de-Boscherville on the edge of Roumare Forest, Saint-Wandrille-de-Fontenelle near Yvetôt, and Jumièges, whose ruins recall the splendours of Romanesque art. Sainte-Marie de Montivilliers is recovering on the banks of the Lézarde, after recent and excellent restoration work, while the Graville Priory, flanked by its black Virgin, overhangs the entrance to Le Havre.

*Le Havre harbour mouth. The town has
regained the status of seaside resort,
and is wearing a new seaside face.
The pebble beach and typical wooden
bathing-huts have been embellished
by a pleasant 'green walk', often crowded
in fine weather. In the background
is the Côte Fleurie (Flower Coast).*

*Following page
Above - A modern version of the
'Terrasse à Sainte-Adresse' pays tribute
to Claude Monet. Below, Le Havre beach,
stretching over two kilometres from the
Pointe de la Hève to the harbour walls.*

*Below - Boulevard Albert I separates the
seafront buildings from the esplanade,
which has a river running through it.*

Founded by François I, Le Havre was devastated during
World War II, and rebuilt by Auguste Perret in the
1950's. The wide avenues at the Porte Océane brighten
up when the light, so admired by the Impressionists,
reflects off the concrete buildings. Thanks to Perret's
techniques, they absorb colour — pink, ochre, grey —
as if trying to rival the neighbouring cliffs in beauty. And
what can you say about the incredible luminosity of
Saint Joseph's Church?

Besides its interesting architecture, Le Havre boasts the
Montgeon Forest on the town heights, the Parc de
Rouelles with its arboretum and dovecote, the Square
Saint-Roch and even a superb Japanese garden offered
by its twin town Osaka.

Several districts of Le Havre have kept their special charm, such as the Saint-François quarter with its Maison de l'Armateur (ship owner's house) and the building containing the Museum of Old Le Havre. Close by, opposite the semaphore, the Malraux Museum holds plenty of art treasures signed Raoul Dufy (born here), Boudin, Monet and Courbet.

The oldest docks in France, shown to advantage by a rehabilitation programme, are part of the lively Eure quarter, and the quays of one of Europe's principal ports are well worth a visit.

The Place Saint-Vincent and its delightful church bring the visitor to the seafront for a two-kilometre stroll.

Previous page - Close-up of Le Havre Town Hall's geometric façade. The 18-floor tower took as many projects before its architect Auguste Perret found the right one. Building started in 1952, and was finished six years later. The pink light, typical of Le Havre's sunsets, illuminates the concrete, as it does to all the western façades of the many 'Perret' buildings in the Town Hall quarter.

The huge Place du Général de Gaulle at Le Havre runs off from the Commerce dock, with its war monument and its 'volcano', the Volcan. This particular cultural structure was strongly criticised at first, but has now joined the ranks of original architectural examples — yet one more for Le Havre.

Company headquarters are multiplying at the entrance to Le Havre: there are already two here in the waters of the Barre docks.

Following page - The Signal, *monumental sculpture by H.G. Adam (1961), in front of the Malraux Museum near the semaphore, which recalls the opening up of the region towards Europe.*

Going back up to Sainte-Adresse, whose 'balmy fragrance of the sea' was praised by Prosper Mérimée in his famous dictation, you cannot miss the landing-stage jumping into the sea, nor the Sugarloaf rising up from the coast to warn sailors. The Dionysians took in Alphonse Karr for a long time; he was 'about as happy at Sainte-Adresse as a man is allowed to be', as he wrote. The tragedian Sarah Bernhardt had a sumptuous residence built there in 1879. Long before this, during her regency, Catherine de Médicis stayed at Vitenval Manor, which is still admired today. There is peace and quiet, as well as pretty houses in this 'Le Havre Nice'.

The way out of Le Havre to the east leads to the Tancarville and Normandy bridges, but you can always avoid the bridges and cross the Seine by ferry, or 'bac', which carries cars and pedestrians from one bank to the other. There are nine in all between Quillebeuf and Grand-Quevilly, and they inspired this witty comment from the comedian Francis Blanche: 'Students, don't present yourselves at the bac (baccalauréat), take the Pont de Tancarville instead'.

Along the roads of the Eure department, it is quite common to see watermills still standing, in the valley towards Louviers or near Pont-de-l'Arche, the only place in Europe to keep mills with a waterwheel. They were needed by local craftsmen in the drapery, metallurgy and paper-making industries.

East of Rouen is the Normandy Vexin, described by Claude Monet as 'splendid country'. The Impressionist painted famous pictures inspired by his Giverny gardens, now a museum. Anatole France appreciated the charms of Vernon: 'It is a small town whose slate roofs go blue in the sunlight, overlooked by a round tower and the three steeples of the old collegiate church'.

The Tancarville Bridge is more than
1 400 metres long and was opened
in 1959. It leads over to the Vernier
marshlands then further on,
to Pont-Audemer in the Eure.

In this part of the department lie the Andelys, birth-place of the artist Nicolas Poussin; a museum marks the event. The finest panoramic view of the Petit-Andely and its meander in the Seine can be seen from the 'year-old daughter'. This is how long it took Richard the Lionheart to build Château-Gaillard, one of the biggest medieval fortresses of its time. Today, it lies in ruins.

The two Cistercian abbeys, Fontaine-Guérard, 20 minutes from Rouen, and Mortemer with its doveco-te and museum of monastic life, are equally fascina-ting. Bordered on the northern side with charming vil-lages around the Lyons Forest and its giant beech-trees, and to the east by the River Epte as far as Gisors, Normandy has found its natural boundaries.

Claude Monet's house at Giverny,
where the painter settled in 1883.
The famous garden where he spent
his time continued to inspire
his work until his death in 1926.

Notre-Dame d'Evreux Cathedral was first built around the time of Rollo the Viking chief's baptism. The cathedral has since been destroyed and rebuilt several times. Opposite is the former XVth century ishop's palace, today the town museum.

Following page - Green hills, chalk cliffs and a loop in the Seine are the backdrop to the Andelys, two villages united in 1791: Petit-Andely and Grand-Andely are separated by a swamp.

The 'road to Louviers' leads on from the ancient fortress Pont-de-l'Arche. This place became known for the manufacture of sheets under Colbert's impetus. The former convent of the Louviers Penitents was the only cloister in Europe built on water.

The Iton valley shelters the departmental capital, Evreux. The town has suffered from war countless times, both in the Middle Ages and during the XXth-century conflicts. Notre-Dame Cathedral has managed to keep its precious XIVth and XVth-centuries glass, however, and is extremely beautiful. The Town Hall, the Tour de l'Horloge (Clock Tower) the former Ursuline convent and the Bishop's Palace (now the town museum) are all carefully preserved monuments. The fountain in the square shows the River Eure transformed into a woman with her two children, the Iton and the Rouloir, at her side.

To the north-west, after le Neubourg and l'Ecorché's amazing anatomical museum, the Château du Champ de Bataille, built in 1651, is a splendid mixture of brick and stone walls, gilded slate roofs and doors and windows of red Chinese lacquer. The 'jardin des Dieux' (Garden of the Gods), set out according to Le Nôtre's plans, contains a giant chessboard, among other things. This prodigious estate is undergoing well-deserved restoration work. Not far away, the Harcourt estate is the ancestral home of one of Normandy's oldest families. The medieval castle is lined with one of the first French arboreta, with hundreds of essential oils. The Château de Beaumesnil dates back almost to the same era: its imposing Baroque façades are mirrored in an ornamental lake. Yet another abbey, Bec-Hellouin with its Saint Nicholas Tower overlooking the abbey buildings, is six kilometres from Brionne.

Previous page - Timeless atmosphere. Encircled by the Risle and the surrounding hills, Pont-Audemer is criss-crossed by rivers jumping under elegant little bridges. It is enviously known as the 'Venice of Normandy'.

One of the most splendid of Normandy's castles is Champ de Bataille, built for the Comte de Créqui in 1651. After Revolutionary pillage it was abandoned until 1948, and is now being constantly renovated. These gold-leaf dolphins are witnesses; they have been playing the fountain in the central lake for several years.

The Romanesque abbey of Notre-Dame-de-Bernay is the oldest in Normandy. Although founded in the XIth century, the passing of time has altered neither its prestige nor its beauty.

In the south of the department, at Verneuil-sur-Avre, some superb wooden houses, turreted and half-timbered, remain from past centuries, round the church and the Place de la Madeleine. Nonancourt marks the southern border with its medieval remains, its half-timbered houses and the octagonal church tower.

'Honfleur, which has a delightful port full of masts and sails, crowned with green hills, surrounded by narrow houses...' wrote Victor Hugo. It is true that these stone and wooden buildings have grown up crowded together around the port of Honfleur.

A stormy sky and contrasting light on the port of Honfleur are sure to inspire the many painters working here. The docks were fitted out by Colbert in 1690.

Following page - Saint Etienne's Church. Built in 1369 on the Quai Saint-Etienne, Honfleur's oldest church is now the Naval Museum (Musée de la Marine).

Alphonse Allais' town continues to inspire painters on the jetty. This jewel of the Calvados department contains the Lieutenance at the far end of the Vieux Bassin (Old Dock), the Maison de l'Armateur (Shipowner's House) on the Quai Saint-Etienne, Saint Catherine's Church with its wooden framework and tower, and two salt lofts in the Enclos quarter. Honfleur has kept up a cultural heritage from two of its sons, in the Maison Satie, devoted to the composer Erik Satie, and the Eugène Boudin Museum.

Previous page
Above - The Lieutenance, already
mentioned in XIth century documents.
A bronze bust of Champlain recalls
his sailing to found Quebec in 1608.

Below - Cobbled streets and uneven slate
house fronts clinging together in the blessed
light of the setting sun. Beautiful Honfleur...

The sun sets, the terraces light up around
the docks. It's 'la dolce vita', Normandy-style.

Deauville and Trouville are like two sisters linked together by a bridge over the Touques. In the XIXth century, the Duc de Morny made a seaside resort from marshland and salt flats; it became one of the most reputed in the world. The modest fishing port of Trouville was similarly launched at full speed into fashion by Alexandre Dumas and his artist friends. Since then, almost everyone has stepped on the famous boardwalks, admired the 300 or so Deauville villas and climbed the steep alleys of Trouville towards the cliff-top.

There is a striking contrast between the seasons - quiet in winter, crowded in summer — yet the charm of these two resorts is always present, as is their rivalry: each in its own way must be more elegant, more sophisticated.

Previous page - The art galleries of the Place Sainte-Catherine, and the medieval church with its separate wooden tower, the only one of its kind left in France.

Superb panoramic view of Trouville and Deauville from the Bon Secours Cross.

At Trouville near the sea, the Art-Deco bathing huts of local architect Maurice Halley and the 1912 casino blend in well with the trawlers and mackerel cargoes filling the port.

The boardwalks are lined with impressive villas, but Trouville also knows how to be discreet. The Escalier du Serpent (Snake Steps) more often known as the Escalier des Cent Marches (Hundred Steps) is typical: almost two kilometres of passages winding up to the town heights, after hidden architectural treasures.

Previous page - Day's end at Trouville.
Parasols and deckchairs are folded up;
the beach is deserted and the light sublime.

The Trouville planks date from 1868.
This elegant boardwalk along the coast is
lined with massive villas in seaside style.

The world's stars stay in the luxury Royal and Normandy Hotels, nestling beside the casino opposite the more recent Deauville International Centre. Among other events, the resort has gained an international reputation for its American Film Festival, now an institution.

Deauville also impresses the world of the turf, with its two racecourses, the Anglo-Norman style buildings of La Touques and the half-timbered stables at Clairfontaine. Up in the town heights, the Strassburger villa is one of the region's most beautiful houses. It belonged to Gustave Flaubert's family, then to a Baron de Rothschild before being sold to a rich American, but was donated to the town in 1980 and is now listed. Far from the madding crowd, the Calouste Gulbenkian Park provides a perfect setting redolent of rare essences.

Light and shadows play on the legendary Deauville boardwalk.

Following page
Above - Deauville's many quaint half-timbered houses, near the market-place.

Below - Evening splendour and high-jinks at Deauville. The first casino opened in 1864, followed by a second in 1912. The architect Georges Wybo designed his building in XVIIIth-century style.

Lisieux is the heart of the Auge country and the sous-préfécture of the Calvados department. The town is known for Thérèse Martin or Saint Thérèse of Lisieux as she became once beatified.

Apart from the basilica, the city contains a cathedral and a Bishop's Palace. Not far away, the beautiful abbey of Saint-Pierre-sur-Dives is worth looking out for.

Previous page – Deauville. Silhouette of a beach star against the light, with parasol.

The basilica of Sainte-Thérèse-de-Lisieux. Pope Pius XI had the first stone laid in September 1929 in memory of Sister Thérèse of the Infant Jesus, a young Carmelite from Normandy. Pilgrims come in their thousands to visit the basilica, a blend of Romanesque and Byzantine styles, and to follow the Way of the Cross.

Cabourg, beauty-spot on the Côte Fleurie,
with its traditional blue-and-white striped
bathing cabins lined up on the sand
in fine weather.

Following page
Above - The castle and church at Caen,
feudal temples, used to look down at
lords and vassals going past on foot or by
carriage. Now they watch the tram slide
silently by. It has only been in service
since 2002.

Below - Calm waters in
the sailing harbour at Caen.

When he came to Cabourg 'in remembrance of things past', Marcel Proust hadn't yet re-named it Balbec. The author found peace and quiet near the Grand Hôtel, and its 'Romantics' Beach'.

At the confluence of the Rivers Odon and Orne lies Caen, the capital of Lower Normandy developed by William the Conqueror. This city too was rebuilt after being almost wiped out during the last war.

However, some of the monuments built for the duke-king can still be seen. The Abbaye aux Hommes (Men's Abbey), today the Town Hall, is surprisingly splendid with its graceful mixture of styles. As if in answer, the Abbaye aux Dames (Ladies' Abbey) is now the seat of the Regional Council. It was built for Queen Matilda, who is buried in La Trinité Church, and its formal gardens, fountains, monumental staircase and crypt complete yet another majestic site. One of the most typical buildings in Caen is the Renaissance Hôtel d'Escoville.

In the Rue Saint-Pierre, Rue Caponière and Rue Froide, the period houses are built of Caen stone or half-timbered. Some are undergoing meticulous restoration work, such as the ancestral house of the Quatrans. Other old buildings may be found in the Vaugueux quarter, renowned for both its architecture and its restaurants. Nearby, the ducal castle contains the Normandy and Fine Arts Museums. The Exchequer Room and Saint George's Church are conserved there, and attract a great number of tourists.

The Caen Memorial stands on the Eisenhower Esplanade, named after the Allied Commander of the D-Day forces. It was put up in 1988 to commemorate both the Normandy Landings and the history of the XXth century. This cultural centre, dedicated to international peace, was the scene of the official reconciliation between Jacques Chirac and Gerard Schröder on 6 June 2004, sixty years after D-Day.

Previous page
Above - The Abbaye aux Hommes,
with the abbey church of Saint Etienne
beside it. Inside is the tomb
of William the Conqueror.

Below - View of the abbey, with the Town
Hall and part of the gardens, beautifully-lit.

The Caen Memorial, designed by the
architect Jacques Millet, was opened on
6 June 1988 and extended in 2002.
Neither a monument nor a museum,
the Memorial aims to provoke thoughts
about peace, and its fragility.

Close by, the 'colline aux oiseaux' (Birds' Hill) is a vast floral park stretching over 17 hectares, and built on what used to be a refuse tip. The park was opened in 1994, and today is a multicoloured universe with 15 000 varieties in its rose garden. It also contains several other types of garden, and a maze. Other green spaces have been kept up in Caen, and its citizens are equally proud of their urban prairie and their racecourse.

William the Conqueror was born in Falaise. The Duke of Normandy had a castle built above this historic town, and liked to come back to it, even after being crowned King of England. The castle fell into ruins, but has now been restored, allowing it to be visited again.

Normandy's history is once again the subject at Bayeux, where the celebrated linen canvas embroidered in wool tells the story of William the Conqueror's combat between 1064 and 1066. The Bayeux Tapestry is over 70 metres long, and is an artistic as well as a historic treasure, miraculously preserved since the Middle Ages.

Previous page - The cloister and gardens of the Abbaye aux Hommes set off the Town Hall. The original convent buildings were built around the cloister, but were later destroyed during the Wars of Religion, then put up again in the XVIIIth century.

William the Conqueror's castle, planted on a rock overhanging the Ante valley at Falaise. This plain, geometric building has been protecting the town for a thousand years.

There are cemeteries, memorials, museums and monuments to Operation Overlord aplenty between Ouistreham and Sainte-Mère-Eglise. A replica of Pegasus Bridge spans the Caen Canal at Bénouville.

The imposing manor-farms that can be seen as far as Isigny, then again in the Manche, are a sign of the region's wealth.

The Orne's bucolic scenery contains its own architectural treasures. Castles, manors, keeps and dovecotes aplenty are to be discovered from the top of a slope, or coming round a hill.

The American cemetery at Colleville, consecrated in 1956. France gave 70 hectares to the United States in memory of the soldiers who died on 6 June 1944. Above Omaha Beach, 9,387 marble crosses are lined up near the Garden of the Departed.

Following page - A close-up view of the Château du Breuil with its half-timbering and pink tiles, on the edge of the Touques a few kilometres from Pont-l'Evêque.

Argentan is the department's sous-préfécture. Birthplace of the painter Fernand Léger, the town suffered heavy bombing in the last war, but a few towers escaped, and are still proudly standing, like the superb churches of Saint-Germain and Saint-Martin. De Sées Cathedral was burnt down and rebuilt four times. From a distance, its spires look like two peaks thrusting up from the plain towards the sky.

Thérèse Martin was born at Alençon. She became Saint Thérèse of the Infant Jesus, and her birthplace can still be visited. Like Argentan, the town is famous for its lace-making — the point d'Alençon — and has kept its old-fashioned elegance. The Maison d'Ozé, once inhabited by Charles de Valois, Duke of Alençon and his wife Marguerite d'Angoulème, is well worth a visit. So is the Lace Museum, which, like the Lace House in Argentan, recalls the importance of this regional craft in the XVIIth and XVIIIth centuries.

Notre-Dame d'Alençon, remarkable 'stone lace' church. Saint Thérèse was christened here in 1873.

Following page - Alençon Cornmarket. This round monument was put up in 1806, and today is an exhibition space.

Bagnoles-de-l'Orne is another treasure, set in an emerald jewel-case. In this watering-place, the most illustrious crowned heads once frolicked on the lake; their hotels and luxurious residences can still be seen in the Belle Epoque quarter built in the late XIXth century. Here, the Comtesse de Ségur had her 'General Dourakine' come for treatment. The author herself lived in the Château des Nouettes near L'Aigle, and a fair number of her stories are set in the Orne.

Near the Andaines Forest, not far from 'Swiss Normandy', Flers has a XVIth-century castle in the heart of a park with a pond and a moat around it. Today, the castle contains a museum and the Town Hall.

The XVIth century Château de Flers, in the frozen silence of a winter morning. The headquarters of the Norman Chouans were once here.

Following page
Above - In the green heart of Swiss Normandy, the streams snake and tumble into falls, forming amazing crescents in deep valleys below impressive gorges.

Below - Bagnoles-de-l'Orne, cheerful watering-place in the heart of the Andaines Forest.

Ruins of the Château de Domfront,
built around 1100 by the Lord de Domfront
and King of England, Henry I Beauclerc.

Following page - The XIIIth century
Norman-Gothic de Sées Cathedral,
built on unsteady land.
Strong buttresses had to be added
in the XVIth century to hold it up.

Further south, the medieval town of Domfront on its rocky sandstone peak has kept its ramparts, parts of its defensive towers and its ruined keep. Notre-Dame-sur-l'Eau remains one of the region's finest Romanesque churches with its frescoes, statues, tombstones and the department's only gisant, or recumbent statue.

Further north, Lonlay Abbey's former splendour has been largely destroyed, but the transept with the original capitals remains, as does the church, in a pleasantly rustic setting.

Near the Trappe Forest at Soligny, there is still a monastery on the marshy land where an abbey was built ten centuries ago. The Trappist Order was born here.

Roger Martin du Gard lived at Bellême, and the famous philosopher Alain was born at Mortagne-au-Perche, where a museum contains his furniture and belongings. Also in the Orne, at Nonant-le-Pin, is the birthplace of Alphonsine Plessis, who became Marie Duplessis, Alexandre Dumas fils' notorious 'Lady of the Camelias'. She has her museum a few kilometres away, at Gacé.

In the Cherbourg harbour roads on a
weekday. A port offers many sensations:
you hear the waves breaking on the
harbour walls, the gulls crying,
the low-speed diesel engine of a ship
turning round; you smell the ozone,
the kelp, the low tide, the fresh paint
on a trawler being repaired...

Following page
Above - Pretty 1880's Italian-style
theatre on the Place de Gaulle.

Below - Back view of the submarine
Le Redoutable, launched in 1961,
a 'defence secret' now available
to the public inside the Cite de la Mer
at Cherbourg.

Between the Pointes de Lévy and de Querqueville
stands Cherbourg, with the Roule Fort and the Liberation
Museum overlooking the gulf. The great harbour was
built in the XVIIIth century, and its walls join up with Pelee
Island to the east, and to several forts.

The arsenal is a sign of former military activity, and the
statue of Napoleon 1 recalls the time when this was a
port of war. These words of the Emperor's are engraved
on the statue's plinth: 'I had resolved to renew at
Cherbourg the wonders of Egypt'. In 1860, the ship La
Belle Poule brought back the Emperor's ashes to
Cherbourg. The harbour station, now the Cite de la Mer,
recalls the translantic era and the town's maritime call-
ing. Cherbourg is one of the Cotentin's treasures, thanks
to the careful upkeep of docks and parks.

Above Cherbourg, the Renaissance Chateau des Ravalet
queens it at Tourlaville on the site of an earlier, medieval
castle. A superb landscaped park with lakes and deer
surrounds it.

The pretty town of Valonges is known as the 'Normandy Versailles', and XVIIth and XVIIIth century mansions can still be seen in its streets, along with the ancient seminary, now a high-school, and other stone buildings. The streams are dotted with bridges and washing-places. The Alauna thermal baths are the region's Gallo-Roman remains.

Saint-Lo, in the heart of the Cotentin peninsula, is the prefecture of the Manche department. The town is encircled by ramparts, and several of its towers remain standing, despite heavy World War Two bombing. The belfry, the Poudriere Tower — a vestige of the enclosure put up in the reign of Charlemagne — and the Beaux Regards Tower are among them.

One of Normandy's oldest fairs is held each year at Lessay, on the edge of the moor. The Holy Cross was established in the XIIth century by the monks who built the Benedictine abbey of the Holy Trinity.

Villedieu-les-Poeles is the tin and copper town. Behind the old houses and period courtyards and alleys are workshops and bell foundries. The museums show examples of stove-manufacturing, lace-making and Norman furniture. There is even a 'clock kingdom'.

Previous page - Barfleur Port,
the most important in medieval Cotentin.
The first lifeguard station in France
was created here in 1865, owing to
the many shipwrecks off the coast.

Saint-Lo footbridge, built in 2001.

The tide timetable is essential here.

Following page
Above - At Granville, the Upper Town shelters
the ancient quarters, perched on the rocks
and protected by XVIIth-century ramparts.

Below - Granville port by night; an important
centre for pleasure craft and fishing.

Following double spread - The sky rivals
Mont-Saint-Michel's illuminations in
splendour. This jewel in Normandy's crown
is listed Unesco World Heritage.

During the Hundred Years' War, the Mont Saint Michel (or Saint Michael's Mount) being impregnable, the Englishman Thomas Scales decided to found Granville in 1439, on the land just opposite. The upper town has kept its old quarters high up, with granite houses and walls still visible on the rock when you go up through the Grand'porte, formerly a drawbridge.

In the lower town, on the Plat-Gousset promenade, you can well imagine the buccaneers and terre-neuva explorers who made Granville a maritime community par excellence. Today, sailing and fishing harbours, sea-water therapy clinics and the Regional Nautical Centre confirm that nothing has changed. One last thing; the fashion designer Christian Dior was born here in January 1905. His birthplace is now a museum, set in a superb park.

Chiselled silhouette of the Mont-Saint-Michel projected onto the sand.
The bay is left bare every day when the strongest tide in Europe goes out.

Following page - An architectural masterpiece put up on a granite rock untouched by erosion. First, a monumental church built on the top in 1020 by Benedictine monks, then convent buildings constructed around it up to the XIIIth century. The builders' prowess is emphasised today by a light setting which you cannot help but admire.

Avranches jealously guards a treasure: the Mont-Saint-Michel manuscripts, written on parchment between the VIIIth and XVth centuries and handed in to Avranches Library in 1791. In the town church lies the relic of Saint Aubert, founder of the Mont-Saint-Michel in 708.

Since that date, the Mount has been standing proudly, with a view of several kilometres around.

Parallel to the abbey and its majestic buildings, a walled village was established in the Middle Ages. Every year, more than three million visitors and pilgrims come through the fortified enclosure, the Grande Rue and its shops, the Abbey estate, starting from the former Corps de Garde des Bourgeois (guards' room) which contains the Tourist Office, the Boulevard Gate and the Porte du Roy (King's Gate). An unfloodable dyke built at the end of the XIXth century links the Mont to the mainland.

Coast and Countryside

Who better than Guy de Maupassant, born near Dieppe in the Chateau de Miromesnil, to describe the Normandy landscapes? 'Before us, the Seine stretched out, undulating, closed in by islands, lined on the right with white cliffs crowned by a forest, on the left by immense prairies cut off by another forest right over there'. How green these valleys are — and how rich the colour when the fields are full of ripe wheat, linen and corn!

There are few clos-masures (local farms) still standing in the Caux country, but they are no less typical of the area. The farmhouse and outbuildings are sheltered from the wind by banks of oaks and beeches, and sturdy apple trees stand in the courtyards.

Previous page - Stormy weather in Normandy: sea and sky seem to fight for the light.

This enclosed farm's sunwashed buildings make an attractive contrast to the cloudy sky. They are sheltered from the winds off the Caux plains by banks of oaks and beeches.

*The Seine-Maritime, known for its coastline,
is also a wooded department.
Eawy Forest is one of Europe's
most beautiful beechwoods.*

*Following page
Above - When the spring sky darkens
with heavy cloud, the sun comes down
into the fields of flowering rape,
just like in a painting.*

*Below - A sunbeam lightens the heavy sky,
bathing an isolated building in sunlight
and illuminating the greenery.*

Normandy created the garden of paradise. Around Dieppe, after the hilly routes through the wood and the Vasterival valley, the Princess Sturdza's garden is pure heaven. So is the bois des Moutiers garden, and further south, Giverny, whose walks are full of roses and nasturtiums, clematis, orchids and waterlilies.

Following the Bresle in the north of the Seine-Maritime, Eu Forest links the Vimeu plateau to the Bray country. It stretches over sixty kilometres or so, taking in the valley of the River Epte, and is marked out by its 'buttonhole', a geological depression resulting from the forming of the Alps. From Eawy Forest in the Seine-Maritime to the copses of the Perche and Belleme, Normandy offers superb swathes of green, where a host of wildlife bells, chirps, tweets and cackles.

Round Fecamp, the pays des Hautes-Falaises or High Cliff country, calls up postcard pictures. Normandy has over 600 kilometres of coastline between Le Treport and the Mont-Saint-Michel. These are the highest cliffs in Europe, covered in broom and gorse, with harbours and beaches at their feet, becoming seas of sand towards Granville. Rocks appear as the tides turn. The hiker can follow the smuggler's path — here called the Sentier des Douaniers, or Revenue Men's path — but needs to climb carefully over these fragile cliffs, lashed by wind and waves.

You can also follow the streams and rivers, snaking down to creeks and inlets, home of herring gulls, sea-gulls and cormorants, a few falcons and even a pelican, who has settled on the Antifer headland!

Previous page
Above - Gorse and broom-covered
plateaux, up on the chalky cliffs.

Below - Cliffs at Eu. These chalky
natural monuments are the highest
in Europe, often well over 100 metres.

Stormy sea at Etretat, near
the Porte d'Aval et de l'Aiguille.
The waves wash carelessly over
the pebbles, the better to crash
against the chalk feet of
the 'white mountains'...

Lower down, the Seine Estuary is the most important natural reserve in France. Despite the port industries at Le Havre, the prairies, marshes, reeds, and mudflats are full of exceptional flora and fauna, with some rare species, such as the black-tailed godwit, the avocet and the protected bittern, feeding in its snug reedy refuge. There are also a few Camargue horses, and some West Highland cattle.

Opposite the Chateau de Tancarville and the canal, the Vernier marshes are no longer the swampy lands they used to be. From the Roque headland to Sainte-Opportune-la-Mare and Quillebeuf, the marsh gets its name from the alders, also known as vernes. The thatched cottages begin here, among luxuriant greenery. These typical roofs made of clay and reeds planted with iris, or flag, protect the cob walls, held up with half-timbering.

Reed beds in the Vernier marshes,
both habitat and pantry for the
plentiful fauna.

Following page
Above - Orchards with their apple trees
in blossom. This has to be Normandy.

Below - Norman bocage.
Fields and meadows parcelled up
by hedges form a crazy-paving effect.

Beyond Quilleboeuf, follow the Seine — calmer now since the disappearance of that impressive and danger-ous high-tide wave known as the mascaret — and dream a little in the cosy charm of Vieux-Port. The sur-rounding natural and regional Parc de Brotonne contains 72 towns and villages, on both riverbanks, and its chalky hillsides shelter protected species such as fal-cons and owls, along the Seine Valley.

The forests cover a fifth of the Eure territory. Hedges and lines of 'tadpole' trees are traditional in this part of Normandy, protecting the orchards and separating the fields. In Auge country, delightful streams called douets splash softly through green meadows. Another green paradise can be found towards Le Lieuvin, hemmed in by water, and the Ouche country, with riverfulls of trout, roach and carp.

Previous page - Horseriding along the seafront at Deauville is a common sight. The town is also reputed for its sale of yearlings.

Autumn on the banks of the Seine. In the background is the Brotonne Bridge, spanning the river since 1977.

Going back to the sea, from Honfleur to Houlgate and Cabourg stretches the Cote Fleurie, whose name is a stark contrast to the Vaches Noires (Black Cows) cliffs near Villers-sur-Mer. The Cote de Nacre, or Mother-of-Pearl Coast, is lined with lower cliffs and sandy dunes as far as Courseulles. Waves and currents have worn away the rock to form unique cavities or 'confession-als' between Lion-sur-Mer and Luc-sur-Mer; impressive holes that look like the mouths of giant caves.

In Bessin country, the rich grass of the bocage mingles with the marshes round the estuaries. The Pointe du Hoc juts out to sea while the cliffs dive down to the Veys bay, which hollows out the land between the D-Day beaches as far as Isigny. The bay is an exceptional site, merging the estuaries of the Rivers Vire and Douve, and alternating peat bogs, bocages and marshes over 25 000 hectares. Rare plants and all sorts of animals thrive in the rich, protected environment of this natural park, which covers the Cotentin and Bessin marshlands.

Gatteville Semaphore, a 25 metres high cylindrical tower built in 1774. Today it is a weather station, and also detects marine mammals passing, out at sea.

Following page - The Querqueville Dyke and Fort de l'Ouest, in the Great Harbour at Cherbourg.

Behind Saint-Vaast, the oldest oyster park in Normandy, and next to the Fort de la Hougue, the Saire valley stretches across to Barfleur, with its carefully-preserved sites and a climate so warm that palm-trees and mimosa can be found there.

Near the Cape Levy lighthouse, Fermanville is one of those quiet and pretty villages offering unforgettable walks. Cross one side of the woods to get to the beach, or follow the valley of the Moulins (Windmills) towards the viaduct, rising like a giant in the forest, and the clumps of hydrangeas and lines of stones marking the edges of fields and meadows.

La Hague, which means 'headland' in Scandinavian, is Ireland's twin sister; a wild peninsula full of exceptional flora and fauna and a protected site. Marram grass and red ferns decorate the windblown sand dunes along the Manche department's western coastline. The colours are wonderful, from the white sandbanks to the golden beaches.

The Mortainais offers various samples of landscape — marsh, moor, bocage and forest — on its steep heights, between the snaky See and the wider Selune Valley.

Previous page - La Hague, with its high ancestral rocks of chalk and granite, is a heavenly site. Here, Jean-Francois Millet was born and Jacques Prevert died.

Near the cove of Saint-Martin-sur-La-Hague lies Port Racine, the smallest French port. It is named after a XVIIIth century corsair.

Mont-Saint-Michel Bay is a unique natural phenomenon. Its tides go out as far as 18 kilometres, and come in 'like a galloping horse'; the bay silts up and needs to undergo major work. The rich vegetation in the salt meadows protects herons and wild ducks, and also lambs, whose meat has a special flavour.

Beauty-spots seem to spring up all over the Manche. Between Granville and the Pointe du Roc lie the Chausey Iles, a granite archipelago 'purple with geraniums and fuchsias' according to the writer Roger Vercel. Penguins, seals and dolphins can often be seen frolicking in the strong currents surrounding the islands.

Victor Hugo loved Jersey, 'Isle of flowers', and Guernsey, the two best-known Channel Islands.

Previous page - From time to time, sunset paints a magnificent sky of staggering beauty, like this.

Phantasmagorical atmosphere in the mists of Mont-Saint-Michel; a glowing red sun sets the sand on fire.

Bird colonies of gannets, puffins and guillemots meet herring-gulls, cormorants and herons between Alderney, long, green cliff-lined rock with low banks, the Isle of Tatihou, off the coast at the Pointe de la Hougue, and the Saint-Marcouf islands, furthest from the mainland and aptly nicknamed 'Bird islands'.

The immense bocages and forests, hills and heather-covered moors of the Orne department have inspired countless authors and legends. In the Argentan country, gateway to the Normandy-Maine natural park, the prairies and valleys abound in trout rivers. The Ornais Auge is horse-breeding country, known for its many reputed stud farms.

Goury, hamlet and port, on the Cotentin headland. In the background, the famous lighthouse put up in 1934 800 metres from the mainland scoffs at the dangerous Blanchard currents which give it a rough time.

Following page
Above - The Pin stud-farm, known as 'the Versailles of the horse', was founded in 1715 at the behest of Louis XIV.

Below - Lower Normandy is renowned for its breeding of thoroughbreds and stallions.

Swiss Normandy is a green treasure nesting between Orne and Calvados, with Clecy, its main town, at the heart. Rivers twist and tumble in deep valleys at the foot of impressive gorges like the Saint-Aubert, or the legendary Villiers gorges in the Andaines Forest.

The forests of Ecouves and Perseigne climb along a range over 400 metres high, round Alencon and Carrouges. The Mancelles Alps, with the Mont des Avaloirs rising highest among them, stretch as far as the Sarthe between sharp rock faces and enclosed valleys.

After the region's highest peaks comes the Perche, a wide plateau in the south of the department, whose rich prairies are the home of that famous breed of draught-horse, the percheron. There are fields and prairies as far as the eye can see, clusters of trees like those at Belleme or round Mortagne, sharp rises whose slopes shelter bocages that well deserve protection. The Perche Natural Park was created in 1998.

Generous in every sense, that's Normandy.

Above and following page
'On the horizon, the sky is as red as hell'
(Arthur Rimbaud, in Le Bal des pendus*)*
Sunset on the Channel, a magnificent sight.

Gastronomy

A foodie on a voyage of discovery in the region would be spoilt for choice faced with the diversity of the products. You have to like butter (the Isigny butter has an Appelation d'Origine Controllee) and cream, which has many uses here: it goes in the 'Vallee d'Auge' sauce, for instance. The 'confiture de lait' (milk preserve) should also be tasted.

A gourmet in Normandy's worries start with the huge variety of fish and seafood from the region's coasts. Saint-Jacques scallops, for example, which account for half of French production, and oysters, from Saint-Vaast and the impressive pied-de-cheval (horse's foot) from Courseulles-sur-Mer.

Previous page - Appetising still-life.
The famous tripe 'à la mode
de Caen' (Caen-style).
A delicacy for those in the know.

Revigorating seafood platter,
with a glass of dry white wine.
This classic never goes out of
fashion on the Norman table.

The lobster carefully caught in Cotentin is quite willing to be cooked with sliced carrots and leeks, a little celery and an onion, respecting the traditional recipe 'Demoiselle de Cherbourg a la nage' ('Young Lady from Cherbourg swimming').

There are different ways of eating mussels, but here, of course, they are firstly served with cream. The connoisseur will appreciate hot, cooked prawns in Honfleur, which celebrates that delicious shellfish in October. Dieppe is famous for Sole Normande, coated with cream. The fresh river trout finish en papillotes (baked in foil) with a large spoonful of fresh cream and a few drops of Calvados, sometimes surrounded by finely-sliced apples. The pikeperch, perch, salmon and pike are always welcome on the region's tables.

Saint-Vaast oysters with their 'nutty flavour'. Norman oyster-farmers produce around 30 000 tonnes of oysters a year.

Following page - Composition of Saint-Jacques scallops caught in Normandy. The region accounts for almost half the national production.

In the farmyards, geese and ducks were not originally intended for foie gras, but recently its production has been growing as it becomes increasingly sought-after.

The charitable Norman cow is no longer shown with her tricoloured pelt (blonde, beige or brown) and her 'spectacles'. She provides milk or meat, according to her breed.

Rouennaise duck owes its speciality value to the fact that the bird is suffocated and not bled before cooking. It is served with a blood sauce. As Curnonsky, 'prince of gastronomes', wrote: 'the manner of execution is perhaps a little cruel, but at the first mouthful, one forgives the duck everything'. The recipe persists, and ensures happy customers in the restaurants of Rouen and Duclair.

Lamb raised in the salt meadows of the Mont-Saint-Michel Bay crops grass scented by the sea at the spring tides, which gives it a flavour long since valued beyond the borders of Normandy.

Previous page - Isigny butter has had its AOC since 1986, but its reputation goes back to the XVIth century.

The majestic Norman cow. The rich pasture gives top-quality milk, basis of Normandy's famous milk products, so important to regional gastronomy.

The andouille de Vire (cold sausage) is traditionally hand-made, then smoked over beechwood for eight weeks, and finally soaked, cooked and dried, before being tasted.

The boudin (blood pudding) at Saint-Romain near Le Havre, or Mortagne-au-Perche is delicious eaten on its own, but can be served with apples, like the andouille de Vire.

When cow's stomach tastes good, it's called tripe 'à la mode de Caen'. It has its fans everywhere, and the Brotherhood of the Golden Tripe-Butcher holds a world-wide competition every year. There was also Mother Poulard from the Mont, who beat her eggs in such a way that her recipe is still the last word in omelettes.

Appetising andouille de Vire.
Its skin is black from the smoking,
and striped with string-marks,
having been tied up before
being cooked.

Excellent products prepared by talented and ingenious chefs deserve stars and good marks, and here are a few examples.

In Caen, Sandrine and Ivan Vautier point out that 'great cooking needs great products'. In this way, the XIXth century *Le Pressoir* gained its stars near Bretteville-sur-Odon. On Boulevard Cornuché in Deauville, *L'Etrier* of the Royal Barrière suggests sole with seaweed and Normandy oysters, while whole joints of meat are cooked at low temperature on the piano.

In Rouen, the star-studded chef Gilles Tournadre has settled in on the Quai de la Bourse where he serves slice of turbot, filet of bass, foie-gras in pastry with 'pain d'épices' (gingerbread) and pigeon Rouennaise-style.

Eric Provost at l'Etrier *in Deauville. The chef trained with the top names in gastronomy, like Joël Robuchon, before setting up in Normandy in 1999.*

La Villa restaurant in Le Havre is the most recent on the list, but has already gained its star. Since July 2001, Jean-Luc Tartarin has been able to compose his menus 'like plays for the theatre'.

His poached crayfish, blue lobster with mango and orange juice, fish from the Côte d'Albâtre and calf sweetbreads are well worth coming back for.

The reputation of Normandy's cheeses is widespread beyond French borders. Four of them have an AOC label.

In Upper Normandy, the neufchatel, subtly salted, is usually moulded into a heart, but other shapes can be found. It goes back all the way to the Hundred Years' War.

In the Calvados, two villages have given their name to cheeses. 'Pont-l'évêque' and 'livarot' are soft cheeses with a strong flavour. The second is easily recognised, surrounded by its five sedges, or strips of reed.

A stone has been put up to Marie Harel in Camembert, and a statue at Vimoutiers. This farmer's wife put camembert cheese on the map; today it is one of the most popular French cheeses. Some eat it hot, right out of the embers; others make a sauce with it, to accompany meat.

Three shapes for three of Normandy's cheeses: heart-shaped 'neufchatel', square 'pont-l'eveque' and round 'camembert'.

The 'livarot', also called 'colonel'. Pierre Corneille's brother Thomas was already praising its merits in his time.

The 'pavé d'Auge' and the 'carré de Bray' are two near cousins. The 'boursin' is also one of the region's cheeses, launched by Francois Boursin at Croisy-sur-Eure in 1964, in a dairy he had founded several years previously. Its creator sprinkled garlic and fine herbs into the cream and milk.

The 'petit-suisse', half-way between cheese and dessert, is also from Normandy! Cream was added to curds to make this little marvel, launched by a farmer's wife and commercialised by the famous Charles Gervais.

When it comes to desserts, everyone here knows the pear 'douillons' and the apple 'bourdelots', where the fruit is wrapped in pastry and served hot. The teurgoule is another speciality made with milk, rice, sugar and cinnamon, and a pinch of salt. The falue, typical brioche, used to be served at local celebrations. Normandy's biscuits appeal to the sweet-toothed, who cannot resist 'Mont-Saint-Michel galettes', 'Bayeux sablés' (shortbread) or 'mirlitons' from Pont-Audemer.

Normandy's appetising 'galettes' made from the best Isigny butter.

Normandy's gastronomy includes the art of preparing an apple tart. There are numerous versions, but served 'à la normande' it is warm, covered with creme fraiche and flambeed with Calvados. Sheer happiness.

According to the tradition now threatened by tougher road safety controls, every feast should be punctuated by a 'trou normand' (Norman Hole). In his *Dictionary of the Table*, Bremond calls it 'absorbing a small glass of spirits in the middle of a heavy meal'. The spirits are sure to be Calvados, with maybe a scoop of sorbet floating in it; apple, of course.

*Amazing apple tart, flying
the flag for regional gastronomy.*

*'The apple tree, so common in France,
gives nowhere such beautiful fruit
nor such varied species as on the
coasts of Normandy, where the maritime
winds breathe from the west"
(Bernardin de Saint-Pierre, born in Le Havre
in 1737, in* Studies of Nature*)*

When it isn't being eaten, the apple, Norman fruit par excellence, is transformed into cider — dry or sweet depending on its sugar content — and 'pommeau', for there are countless varieties in the orchard meadows.

In the Manche and the Orne, pears are used in the same way to make 'poiré' (pear cider). The Gauls were already drinking this many centuries ago, so it surely deserves its two AOC. Benedictine must not be left out of Normandy's drinks repertory either. The Fecamp monks began distilling it in the XVIth century, using 27 plants and spices, and the complete recipe is of course still a secret today. The bottle is known to have inspired Gauguin.

Cheers, Normandy!

After fermentation, the apple juice becomes cider, and pear-juice 'poiré' — a popular drink in the bocage.

Following page - 'Calvados' is obtained from distilled cider, then aged in an oak-cask.

Also published by Declics

Portraits of France©

Brittany **Paris**
Burgundy **Provence**
Dordogne
French Riviera **French Heritage**

...and more than 40 books in French on the towns and regions of France

Consult our website www.declics.fr

© **Editions Déclics 2004**
14, rue des Volontaires - 75015 Paris. France
Tel. 33 (1) 53 69 70 00 - **Fax** 33 (1) 42 73 15 24
E-mail : contact@declics.fr

Printed in France by BARNEOUD (53)

Depot legal 3rd quarter 2004
Code ISBN 2-84768-060-8
Code Sodis 9876574

www.declics.fr

The sun sinks below the horizon.
Most of Europe is already in darkness;
now it's Normandy's turn to sleep

Cover - Natural splendour, a wealth
of heritage, modern road systems:
Normandy welcomes you with all her assets.